British Warships & Auxiliaries

(1982/3 Edition)

by Mike Critchley

(2nd Impression)

D0263928

£1.95

RFA Olwen

INTRODUCTION

By Admiral Sir Henry Leach GCB, ADC First Sea Lord

I have great pleasure in writing the foreword for this year's edition of "British Warships and Auxiliaries". This attractive little book was first published in 1979 and last year over 20,000 copies were sold. Although it only covers the Royal Navy, it has an appeal similar to that of Jane's Fighting Ships and its popularity clearly reflects the British interest in their Navy and maritime affairs.

This of course is as it should be for we are an island race with a seafaring background and tradition stretching back over many centuries. Britain is a country dependent on trade for its living, 95% of which moves by sea; we have to import much of our food and essential raw materials in order to survive. In spite of the changes announced in the recent Defence Review, we will still have the strongest Navy after the two super powers and will continue to be the maritime leader of Europe. Our merchant fleet is the fourth largest in the world and contributes about £1,000 million a year to our balance of payments. It has 1400 ships over 1,000 tons and on any one day there are over 800 merchant ships at sea; this is clearly a vital interest to our country which must be properly safeguarded, an important role for the Royal Navy.

But this is only one role of many. The Royal Navy not only has important tasks in war — the strategic nuclear deterrent, the protection of reinforcements and supplies across the Channel and the Atlantic, mine countermeasures to keep our ports and seaways open, support of the American Strike Fleet in the Eastern Atlantic and protection of our sea lines of communication — but also in times of peace and tension for which the presence and flexibility of maritime power is ideally suited. The advantages of seapower have been fully recognised by the Soviets who have built up a huge modern fleet of ships and submarines which goes far beyond the protection of their own relatively small coastline. These forces are deployed throughout the world, often well outside the NATO boundaries seeking areas of weakness which can be exploited to extend the communist ideology and Soviet influence. The free world must be prepared to match these forces wherever they exist and so deter the Soviets from achieving their expansionist ambitions.

To do this we must have the full mix of maritime forces to operate on, under and above the water, using ships, submarines and aircraft. They work as a team as no single vehicle can do all the tasks on its own. Turning to the ships shown in this publication you will perhaps appreciate how very expensive many of them are. A new Type 22 frigate such as HMS BROADSWORD now costs over £120 million. Much of this is devoted to the weapons carried in the ship which, because of the threat, are of necessity highly complex and hence expensive. Defence today is not cheap and we must bear in mind that Russia is prepared to devote a far greater proportion of her gross national product to her armed forces than any other country. Nevertheless there is a limit to how many of

3

these expensive ships we can afford and in the immediate future it is intended to build cheaper, simpler frigates with a more specialised but lesser overall capability to keep the numbers up.

In this era of rapidly changing technology, the complex question of quality versus quantity is typical of the problems which confront the Admiralty Board which is continually striving to get the best value for money and to strike the right balance. Ship and weapon systems take years to develop and procure yet the circumstances governing these decisions and the threats to our country and way of life do not stand still. It is difficult to predict the future accurately and a mistake could have serious consequences. The aim therefore must be to keep as far as possible a balanced fleet with options open to shift the emphasis one way or another in response to changes in requirement as they arise. This excellent book shows the Royal Navy as it is today; I commend it to you.

First Sea Lord

THE ROYAL NAVY

Undoubtedly the 1981 Defence Review has left the Navy reeling. The announcement of the cuts — and the Navy taking the lion's share of them, should doubtless have been expected, bearing in mind the current financial standing of the country. They do, however, have the hall mark of being "rushed through", with the Navy's teeth being slashed today and promises of the tail being reduced tomorrow.

Doubtless readers of this book will agree that "it should not be allowed to happen" — it would be interesting to know if any have written to their MP to tell him! It is amazing how the major decisions are quietly forgotten and our newspapers move on to other topics. Any other organization under such a threat as the '81 defence review poses for the Navy, would mount a long and loud campaign from within — drawing public attention to the problem. In this country, however, things do not happen that way and our services are expectedto get on with the job — quietly. Whilst not advocating completely open government in the Defence world, informed comment from within the service could only serve to alert the public as to where their money should and should not be spent. Whilst Admirals no longer resign when these cuts are announced — they prefer to stay on and "fight their corner" — it is encouraging to see politicians such as our former Navy Minister, Keith Speed, stand up and set the alarm bells ringing — even though it cost him his job.

Taking a critical look at the implications of the Nott review — now that the dust has settled — is worthwhile, especially when looking in the 'small print'.

Probably the two greatest principles established by the review are that our major fleet units are to be our submarines, and that we are to reflect in our Navy the "throw away" world in which we live. Refits and modernisations are almost to be a thing of the past. As at home — we buy a piece of equipment, use it and throw it out when it goes wrong, or is just out of date. So it will be with our fleet — buy a new ship, work it hard until its equipment is obsolete, then invest in the latest new vessel to replace it! Good news for the ship-builders and equipment suppliers but bad for dockyards who have always been required to modify to current standards almost every class of ship built. Many of our older warships today have undergone extensive mid-life modernisations at frightening cost to the budget. Equipment onboard our ships will increasingly be "repaired by replacement" nine times out of ten. It's now cheaper in the long run to buy new than repair the old — a principle in use within the US Navy for some years.

The decision to completely close Chatham Naval Base and run down the Portsmouth yard, will obviously have far-reaching social effects locally, but many observers feel Chatham should have been closed years ago. The decision to close the multi-million pound investment in the Chatham Nuclear Submarine refit complex, however, can only be described as wrong. With the Rosyth yard almost fully committed to Polaris Submarine refits, and Devonport unable to cope with their present submarine workload on schedule, leaving a number of submarines awaiting refit — can hardly be described as a cost-effective way of deploying these expensive vessels. With the Chatham complex closed, the problem can only get worse.

The decision to complete three of the Invincible Class but only operate two is not surprising. If the third unmanned ship is to be sold is not clear — it may well be that our own reserve fleet could be boosted by one vessel as the number of overseas countries that both want and can afford such a ship are indeed limited. In a time of tension such a ship waiting in the wings could be the answer to many a Royal Marine's prayer. With their assault ships planned to be taken away from them, a ship of Invincible size could be of much more use to them than the cross-channel ferries they are planned to rely on to move manpower and machinery overseas in future years — and ferries cannot operate helicopters!

Submarines — Mr. Nott's answer for our Navy. Admittedly now the capital ships of our fleet have an excellent anti-ship & anti-submarine capability, but there are many roles a submarine cannot fulfil, especially in peacetime, that are undertaken by the workhorse of the Fleet — the frigate! Undoubtedly some of the Navy's commitments will have to be reduced as the size and shape of the Fleet is altered. It will be interesting to see which commitments go.

From the wording of the Defence Review the casual observer would think the conventional submarine replacement was to go ahead — at last! But reading the small print it is clear that despite assurances that the government is pushing ahead with the plan, still no firm orders have been given to any shipbuilder for the planned Type 2400 conventional submarine.

The Surface Fleet
Readers will see from the rest of the book that many ships are to be 'retired early' or placed on the disposal list. Admittedly it still leaves a force to be reckoned with, but bearing in mind the number of ships out of action for ever essential maintenance and repairs, the numbers are small — and numbers at sea are what count. It is interesting to note that two County Class may be converted to Minelayers (a much needed requirement in the Fleet) and they could doubtless double up as Dartmouth training ships in peacetime. With the number of Leander Class to be converted to carry Sea Wolf now reduced, and more heading for the Standby Squadron (to be moved to Portsmouth when Chatham closes) the design work on the new Type 23 is a high priority. The requirement for a number of cheap, reasonably well equipped frigates is urgent. The decision to go for quantity in ships rather than quality has been made. As an interim measure a re-build of more of the highly successful Amazon Class would seem a sensible cost effective way out. They would, of course, have to be equipped with the latest technology rather than their present armament.

Mine Counter Measure Forces
If the Navy has had value for money from any one class of ship, it must be the aged Coastal Minesweeper, which for over twenty years has fulfilled many roles around the world. Their replacements are as expensive as are the sophistication of the mines that could be laid around our shores. It would seem we have to pay up if we are to have any credible mine clearance capability. As an island nation and the world's largest importer of food, let alone raw materials, we disregard the mine — so easily laid off our major ports — at our peril. Mine warfare must become a higher priority for our Navy than it has been in the past. Any RNR man will agree, but they must still wait for their replacement MCMV vessels too — and the money just is not there at present. At last the Hong Kong Patrol vessels are to be replaced, and with a fair sized ship too. With the Hong Kong Government footing 75% of the bill there can be few Treasury complaints.

Survey Fleet
A cinderella service but one that has an important defence and commercial rôle to play. Ships are getting old — the inshore ships particularly — and time spent surveying is reduced as these ships have more and more to be given

'Fleet tasks'. With less than 30% of the UK continental shelf surveyed to modern standards, an ageing fleet and an inadequate replacement programme, the situation is not far short of scandalous. A subject for debate however is whether the Survey Fleet should be funded from a naval vote — or be a Department of Trade responsibility. If the latter there would certainly be more cash available for "front line" warships and aircraft.

Experimental Vessels
It would appear that 'Speedy' has lived up to her maker's specifications, even if some sea states have proved too much for her. It will be interesting to see if the hydrofoil concept is taken up for other ships. The poor old hovercraft, however, seem to have been quietly forgotten — hovercraft trials must be the Navy's longest run evaluation. It must now be time to develop them further or forget the idea completely.

Royal Fleet Auxiliary have suffered their cuts too — smaller ships have been deleted and vessels of the Ness and Tide classes being retired. It is interesting to see the 'redundant' vessels being chartered/sold to the US Navy Military Sealift Command. We can expect to see further RFA/USN co-operation in future years.

Training — the defence review of '81 indicates that more training will be carried out afloat. The ships of the RFA could well be used for this new rôle, and in fact the complete manning of the RFA by RN personnel cannot be ruled out, but the decision to do so would be fought hard by the RFA — let alone the Seamen's Union! Where more training afloat could be carried out must surely be in some non-specialist ships of the RMAS. The basic skills of seamanship and navigation can be learnt by both officers and ratings as easily in, perhaps, an Armament Carrier or TRV around our coast as in a highly expensive frigate — the vessel thus fulfilling two useful rôles. At least this would leave a smaller requirement for space in warships to train men in specialist tasks such as Sonar, Missiles, Communications, etc.

Speaking in the House of Commons recently, Taunton's M.P. (Mr. Edward du Cann) stated that, "I reflect that a few tens of enemy submarines at sea in 1945 required no fewer than 5,000 escorts to counter them. The Russians now have 400 submarines and search at sea is an extremely complex and difficult matter. Even to find one terrorist on land may require 1,000 policemen. In the face of this great advance by the Soviet Union, we have the smallest fleet that we have had for 300 years. Nor do we have the reserves of seamen and merchant ships, which might be the potential escorts of the future, that we had in 1939. The cash may be increasing but our defence general capacity is reducing all the time."

Whichever way the Navy goes — in future years — despite this warning, remains to be seen. It will take time to sort out the seemingly "panic measures" of the '81 review. What is for sure is that we are rapidly approaching the date when, if the nation decides the priority of our Naval forces is so low, we will have reduced our Navy to the size of a fourth division "banana republic". There seems to be an increasingly loud body of opinion who would relish just that. If it happened — God forbid — anyone who cared for the long term security of this, our island nation, must surely keep fingers — and toes even — firmly crossed as they go about their daily tasks in this unsettled world. Our Navy is not cheap, but if we want the insurance policy we have to pay the premiums.

SHIPS OF THE ROYAL NAVY — PENNANT NUMBERS

Ship	Penn. No.	Ship	Penn. No.
Aircraft Carriers		PHOEBE	F42
INVINCIBLE	R05	TORQUAY	F43
ILLUSTRIOUS	R06	MINERVA	F45
ARK ROYAL	R09	DANAE	F47
HERMES	R12	JUNO	F52
		ARGONAUT	F56
Destroyers		ANDROMEDA	F57
KENT	D12	HERMIONE	F58
LONDON	D16	JUPITER	F60
ANTRIM	D18	BACCHANTE	F69
GLAMORGAN	D19	APOLLO	F70
FIFE	D20	SCYLLA	F71
NORFOLK	D21	ARIADNE	F72
BRISTOL	D23	CHARYBDIS	F75
SHEFFIELD	D80	BROADSWORD	F88
BIRMINGHAM	D86	BATTLEAXE	F89
NEWCASTLE	D87	BRILLIANT	F90
GLASGOW	D88	BRAZEN	F91
EXETER	D89	BOXER	F92
SOUTHAMPTON	D90	BEAVER	F93
NOTTINGHAM	D91	YARMOUTH	F101
LIVERPOOL	D92	LOWESTOFT	F103
MANCHESTER	D95	DIDO	F104
GLOUCESTER	D96	ROTHESAY	F107
EDINBURGH	D97	LONDONDERRY	F108
YORK	D98	LEANDER	F109
CARDIFF	D108	AJAX	F114
COVENTRY	D118	ASHANTI	F117
		ESKIMO	F119
Frigates		GURKHA	F122
AURORA	F10	ZULU	F124
ACHILLES	F12	PLYMOUTH	F126
EURYALUS	F15	PENELOPE	F127
DIOMEDE	F16	RHYL	F129
GALATEA	F18	NUBIAN	F131
CLEOPATRA	F28	TARTAR	F133
ARETHUSA	F38	AMAZON	F169
NAIAD	F39	ANTELOPE	F170
SIRIUS	F40	ACTIVE	F171

Ship	Penn. No.	Ship	Penn. No.
AMBUSCADE	F172	**Assault Ships**	
ARROW	F173	FEARLESS	L10
ALACRITY	F174	INTREPID	L11
ARDENT	F184		
AVENGER	F185	**Minesweepers &**	
		Minehunters	
Submarines		ST DAVID	M07
PORPOISE	S01	VENTURER	M08
SEALION	SO7	BRECON	M29
WALRUS	SO8	LEDBURY	M30
OBERON	SO9	CATTISTOCK	M31
ODIN	S10	COTTESMORE	M32
ORPHEUS	S11	BROCKLESBY	M33
OLYMPUS	S12	MIDDLETON	M34
OSIRIS	S13	DULVERTON	M35
ONSLAUGHT	S14	CHIDDINGFORD	M36
OTTER	S15	HURWORTH	M37
ORACLE	S16	ALFRISTON	M1103
OCELOT	S17	BICKINGTON	M1109
OTUS	S18	BILDESTON	M1110
OPOSSUM	S19	BRERETON	M1113
OPPORTUNE	S20	BRINTON	M1114
ONYX	S21	BRONINGTON	M1115
RESOLUTION	S22	WILTON	M1116
REPULSE	S23	CRICHTON	M1124
RENOWN	S26	CUXTON	M1125
REVENGE	S27	BOSSINGTON	M1133
CHURCHILL	S46	GAVINTON	M1140
CONQUEROR	S48	HODGESTON	M1146
COURAGEOUS	S50	HUBBERSTON	M1147
DREADNOUGHT	S101	IVESTON	M1151
VALIANT	S102	KEDLESTON	M1153
WARSPITE	S103	KELLINGTON	M1154
SCEPTRE	S104	KIRKLISTON	M1157
SPARTAN	S105	LALESTON	M1158
SPLENDID	S106	MAXTON	M1165
TRAFALGAR	S107	NURTON	M1166
SOVEREIGN	S108	POLLINGTON	M1173
SUPERB	S109	SHAVINGTON	M1180
SWIFTSURE	S126	SHERATON	M1181

Ship	Penn. No.	Ship	Penn. No.
UPTON	M1187	YARNTON	P1096
WALKERTON	M1188	DEE	P3014
WOTTON	M1195	DROXFORD	P3113
SOBERTON	M1200		
STUBBINGTON	M1204	**Minelayer**	
LEWISTON	M1208	ABDIEL	N21
CROFTON	M1216		
		Survey Ships & RN	
Inshore		**Manned Auxiliaries**	
Minsweepers		BRITANNIA	A00
AVELEY	M2002	ECHO	A70
DITTISHAM	M2621	ENTERPRISE	A71
FLINTHAM	M2628	EGERIA	A72
THORNHAM	M2793	MANLEY	A92
		MENTOR	A94
Patrol Craft		MILLBROOK	A97
ALERT	P252	MESSINA	A107
VIGILANT	P254	HECLA	A133
LEEDS CASTLE	P258	HECATE	A137
KINGFISHER	P260	HERALD	A138
CYGNET	P261	HYDRA	A144
PETEREL	P262	ENDURANCE	A171
SANDPIPER	P263	WAKEFUL	A236
DUMBARTON		BULLDOG	A317
CASTLE	P265	BEAGLE	A319
SCIMITAR	P271	FOX	A320
CUTLASS	P274	FAWN	A335
SABRE	P275	WOODLARK	M2780
ANGLESEY	P277	CHALLENGER	K07
ALDERNEY	P278		
JERSEY	P295		
SPEEDY	P296	**KEEP RIGHT UP TO DATE**	
GUERNSEY	P297		
SHETLAND	P298		
ORKNEY	P299		
LINDISFARNE	P300		
BEACHAMPTON	P1007		
MONKTON	P1055		
WASPERTON	P1089		
WOLVERTON	P1093		

KEEP RIGHT UP TO DATE

The 1983 edition of this book will be available in Nov 1982.

If you wish to be informed when it is available write to:—
Maritime Books, Duloe, Liskeard, Cornwall.

HMS Revenge

RESOLUTION CLASS

Ship	Pennant Number	Completion Date	Builder
RESOLUTION	S22	1967	Vickers
REPULSE	S23	1968	Vickers
RENOWN	S26	1968	C. Laird
REVENGE	S27	1969	C. Laird

Displacement 8,400 tons (submerged) **Dimensions** 130m x 10m x 9m **Speed** 25 knots **Armament** 16 Polaris Missiles, 6 Torpedo Tubes **Complement** 147 (x 2).

Notes

Carrier of the British Nuclear Deterrent, Polaris submarines can fire their missiles from the ocean depths and obliterate a target 2,500 miles away. Each submarine has two crews so that the maximum use can be made of each boat. There is always one, and often two, Polaris submarines at sea on patrol — the area of which is a closely guarded secret — most of the crew do not even know. Their endurance is virtually limitless, having to return to harbour only to replenish food and to give the crew leave. Design work now underway on their replacements — to carry the Trident's missile.

S U B M A R I N E S

11

HMS Courageous

VALIANT CLASS

Ship	Pennant Number	Completion Date	Builder
CHURCHILL	S46	1970	Vickers
CONQUEROR	S48	1971	C. Laird
COURAGEOUS	S50	1971	Vickers
DREADNOUGHT	S101	1963	Vickers
VALIANT	S102	1966	Vickers
WARSPITE	S103	1967	Vickers

Displacement 4,900 tons dived **Dimensions** 87m x 10m x 8m
Speed 28 knots + **Armament** 6 Torpedo Tubes.
Complement 103 (Dreadnought 90)

Notes
DREADNOUGHT was the forerunning of this class, built with an American reactor, and differs slightly to the rest of the class. These boats are capable of high underwater speeds and can remain on patrol almost indefinitely. They are able to circumnavigate the world without surfacing.

HMS Swiftsure

SWIFTSURE CLASS

Ship	Pennant Number	Completion Date	Builder
SCEPTRE	S104	1978	Vickers
SPARTAN	S105	1979	Vickers
SPLENDID	S106	1980	Vickers
SOVEREIGN	S108	1974	Vickers
SUPERB	S109	1976	Vickers
SWIFTSURE	S126	1973	Vickers

Displacement 4,500 tons dived **Dimensions** 83m x 10m x 8m **Speed** 30 knots + dived **Armament** 5 Torpedo Tubes. **Complement** 116.

Notes

A follow-on class of ships from the successful Valiant Class. These submarines have an updated Sonar and Torpedo system and are the very latest in submarine design. A new class of up-dated Swiftsure Class are under construction. The first HMS TRAFALGAR was launched in 1981. HM Ships TURBULENT & TIRELESS and at least two others will follow.

HMS Sealion

PORPOISE CLASS

Ship	Pennant Number	Completion Date	Builder
PORPOISE	S01	1958	Vickers
SEALION	S07	1961	C. Laird
WALRUS	S08	1961	Scotts

Displacement 2,410 tons (submerged) **Dimensions** 90m x 8m x 5m **Speed** 12 knots surfaced, 17 submerged **Armament** 8 Torpedo Tubes **Complement** 70.

Notes

Diesel electric powered submarines that were the first submarines to be designed and built after the war. Capable of long underwater patrols, but mainly used for exercise and training purposes as more Nuclear submarines join the Fleet. The 1981 Defence review stated "We will proceed as fast as possible with a new and more effective class to replace our ageing diesel-powered submarines". This will be the Vickers Type 2400 — now long awaited — but still not ordered.

HMS Onyx

OBERON CLASS

Ship	Pennant Number	Completion Date	Builder
OBERON	S09	1961	Chatham D'yard
ODIN	S10	1962	C. Laird
ORPHEUS	S11	1960	Vickers
OLYMPUS	S12	1962	Vickers
OSIRIS	S13	1964	Vickers
ONSLAUGHT	S14	1962	Chatham D'yard
OTTER	S15	1962	Scotts
ORACLE	S16	1963	C. Laird
OCELOT	S17	1964	Chatham D'yard
OTUS	S18	1963	Scotts
OPOSSUM	S19	1964	C. Laird
OPPORTUNE	S20	1964	Scotts
ONYX	S21	1967	C. Laird

Displacement 2,410 tons (submerged) **Dimensions** 90m x 8m x 5m **Speed** 12 knots surface, 17 knots submerged **Armament** 8 Torpedo Tubes **Complement** 70.

Notes
Very similar to Porpoise Class. Upper casing is made of glass fibre — the first time plastics have been used in submarine construction.

HMS Hermes

HERMES CLASS

Ship	Pennant Number	Completion Date	Builder
HERMES	R12	1959	Vickers

Displacement 28,700 tons **Dimensions** 227m x 27m x 9m **Speed** 28 knots **Armament** 2 Sea Cat Missile Systems, 9 Sea King helicopters, 5 Sea Harrier aircraft, 2 Wessex helicopters **Complement** 980 + aircrews.

Notes
A former fixed wing aircraft carrier converted to a Commando Carrier in 1971-73. Refitted again in 1976 into an Anti-submarine Carrier. Completed further refit in 1981 (for Sea Harrier operations). Flagship for the Falkland Islands Task Force. Due to be sold/scrapped as a defence economy.

HMS Invincible

INVINCIBLE CLASS

Ship	Pennant Number	Completion Date	Builder
INVINCIBLE	RO5	1979	Vickers
ILLUSTRIOUS	RO6	1982	Swan-Hunter
ARK ROYAL	RO9		Swan-Hunter

Displacement 19,500 tons **Dimensions** 206m x 32m x 6.5m
Speed 28 knots **Armament** Sea Dart Missile System
Aircraft: 5 x Sea Harrier, 10 x Sea King **Complement** 900 +
aircrews.

Notes

First of a new generation of mini-aircraft carriers long awaited
by the Royal Navy to provide air cover for a task group of ships.
A "ski ramp" is fitted onto the bow of each ship to enable the
Sea Harrier a greater payload on take-off. Emergency accom-
modation available to enable a full R.M. Commando to be
carried and landed ashore. As a result of the '81 Defence
Review the Royal Australian Navy have purchased INVINCIBLE
for delivery in 1983.

HMS Fearless

FEARLESS CLASS

Ship	Pennant Number	Completion Date	Builder
FEARLESS	L10	1965	Harland & Wolff
INTREPID	L11	1967	J. Brown

Displacement 12,500 tons, 19,500 (flooded) **Dimensions** 158m x 24m x 8m **Speed** 20 knots **Armament** 4 Sea Cat Missile Systems, 2 x 40mm guns **Complement** 580.

Notes

Multi-purpose ships that can operate helicopters for embarked Royal Marine Commandos. 4 landing craft are carried on an internal deck and are flooded out when ship docks down. One ship is usually in refit/reserve. The other is used to train young officers from the RN College, Dartmouth (currently FEARLESS), but still retains amphibious capabilities. Can embark 5 Wessex helicopters. Both ships were reprieved from the scrapman — and rapidly sailed with the Falkland Islands Task Force.

HMS Bristol

BRISTOL CLASS (Type 82)

Ship	Pennant Number	Completion Date	Builder
BRISTOL	D23	1972	Swan Hunter

Displacement 6,750 tons **Dimensions** 154m x 17m x 7m **Speed** 30 knots + **Armament** 1 x 4.5″ gun, Ikara Anti-submarine Missile System, 1 Sea Dart Missile System, 2 x 20mm guns **Complement** 407.

Notes
Eight ships of this class were envisaged. Four were ordered but three later cancelled when requirement for large escorts for fixed wing aircraft carriers ceased to exist. Helicopter Deck provided but no aircraft normally carried. Now used as a Flagship.

19

HMS Antrim

COUNTY CLASS

Ship	Pennant Number	Completion Date	Builder
KENT	D12	1963	Harland & Wolff
LONDON	D16	1963	Swan Hunter
ANTRIM	D18	1970	Fairfield
GLAMORGAN	D19	1966	Vickers
FIFE	D20	1966	Fairfield
NORFOLK	D21	1970	Swan Hunter

Displacement 6,200 tons **Dimensions** 159m x 16m x 6m, **Speed** 32 knots **Armament** 2 x 4.5″ guns, 2 x 20mm guns, 4 Exocet Missiles, 1 x Sea Slug Missile System **Complement** 471.

Notes
KENT and LONDON have 2 extra 4.5″ guns and no Exocet missile systems. Each ship has a Wessex Mk 3 helicopter embarked. KENT is used as a Harbour Training Ship at Portsmouth (future uncertain). LONDON to be sold to Pakistan and NORFOLK to Chile in 1982.

HMS Southampton

SHEFFIELD CLASS (Type 42)

Ship	Pennant Number	Completion Date	Builder
SHEFFIELD	D80	1974	Vickers
BIRMINGHAM	D86	1976	C. Laird
NEWCASTLE	D87	1978	Swan Hunter
GLASGOW	D88	1978	Swan Hunter
EXETER	D89	1980	Swan Hunter
SOUTHAMPTON	D90	1981	Vosper T.
NOTTINGHAM	D91	1982	Vosper T.
LIVERPOOL	D92	1982	C. Laird
MANCHESTER	D95	Building	Vickers
GLOUCESTER	D96	Building	Vosper T.
EDINBURGH	D97	Building	C. Laird
YORK	D98	Building	Swan Hunter
CARDIFF	D108	1979	Vickers
COVENTRY	D118	1978	C. Laird

Displacement 3,660 tons **Dimensions** 125m x 15m x 7m **Speed** 30 knots + **Armament** 1 x 4.5″ gun, 2 x 20mm guns, Sea Dart Missile System: Lynx Helicopter. 6 Torpedo Tubes. **Complement** 280.

Notes
The first class of ships to be equipped with the Sea Dart missile system. Are replacing the County Class in the Fleet. Will not now undergo "mid-life" modernisation.

HMS Brilliant

BROADSWORD CLASS (Type 22)

Ship	Pennant Number	Completion Date	Builder
BROADSWORD	F88	1978	Yarrow
BATTLEAXE	F89	1980	Yarrow
BRILLIANT	F90	1981	Yarrow
BRAZEN	F91	1982/3	Yarrow
BOXER	F92	Building	Yarrow
BEAVER	F93	Building	Yarrow

Displacement 3,860 tons **Dimensions** 131m x 15m x 4m **Speed** 29 knots **Armament** 4 Exocet Missiles, 2 Sea Wolf Missile Systems, 2 x 20mm guns, 6 Torpedo Tubes, 2 Lynx helicopters **Complement** 224.

Notes

Designed as eventual replacements for the Leander Class frigates. The first ship was laid down in 1975 — the last in 1979. An order for a seventh ship placed late 1981.

THE NEW LOOK LEANDERS . . .

HMS ANDROMEDA
after major 'Sea Wolf' rebuilding

F57

HMS Achilles

LEANDER CLASS

Ship	Pennant Number	Completion Date	Builder
ACHILLES	F12	1970	Yarrow
DIOMEDE	F16	1971	Yarrow
JUNO	F52	1967	Thornycroft
● ANDROMEDA	F57	1968	HM Dockyard Portsmouth
● HERMIONE	F58	1969	Stephen
● JUPITER	F60	1969	Yarrow
BACCHANTE	F69	1969	Vickers
APOLLO	F70	1972	Yarrow
● SCYLLA	F71	1970	HM Dockyard Devonport
ARIADNE	F72	1972	Yarrow
● CHARYBDIS	F75	1969	Harland & Wolff

Displacement 2962 tons **Dimension** 113m x 13m x 5m
Speed 27 knots **Armament** 2 x 4.5″ guns, 2 x 20mm guns,
1 Sea Cat Missile System, 1 Mortar Mk 10, 1 Wasp helicopter.
Complement 260.

Only ships marked ● will now be converted to carry the Sea Wolf missile system. JUNO will eventually replace TORQUAY as a Training Ship.

HMS Ajax

LEANDER CLASS (Ikara Conversions)

Ship	Pennant Number	Completion Date	Builder
AURORA	F10	1964	J. Brown
EURYALUS	F15	1964	Scotts
GALATEA	F18	1964	S. Hunter
ARETHUSA	F38	1965	Whites
●NAIAD	F39	1965	Yarrow
DIDO	F104	1963	Yarrow
LEANDER	F109	1963	Harland & Wolff
AJAX	F114	1963	C. Laird

Displacement 2,860 tons **Dimensions** 113m x 12m x 5m **Speed** 29 knots **Armament** 1 Ikara Anti Submarine Missile, 2 x 40mm guns, 2 Sea Cat Missile Systems, 1 Mortar Mk 10, 1 Wasp helicopter **Complement** 240.

Notes

All ships were converted (1973-76) to carry the Ikara Anti submarine Missile System (forward of the bridge) in lieu of a 4.5″ gun. The Wasp helicopter is being replaced in all ships by the Lynx. ● To Disposal List 1982.

HMS Phoebe

LEANDER CLASS (Exocet Conversions)

Ship	Pennant Number	Completion Date	Builder
CLEOPATRA	F28	1966	HM Dockyard Devonport
SIRIUS	F40	1966	HM Dockyard Portsmouth
PHOEBE	F42	1966	Stephens
MINERVA	F45	1966	Vickers
DANAE	F47	1967	HM Dockyard Devonport
ARGONAUT	F56	1967	Hawthorn Leslie
PENELOPE	F127	1963	Vickers

Displacement 2,860 tons **Dimensions** 113m x 12m x 5m **Speed** 27 knots **Armament** 4 Exocet Missiles, 3 Sea Cat Missile Systems, 2 x 40mm guns, 6 Torpedo Tubes, 1 Lynx helicopter **Complement** 230.

Notes
The highly successful Leander Class are the last steam powered frigates in the Royal Navy, all later ships being propelled by gas turbines.

HMS Ambuscade

AMAZON CLASS (Type 21)

Ship	Pennant Number	Completion Date	Builder
AMAZON	F169	1974	Vosper T.
ANTELOPE	F170	1975	Vosper T.
ACTIVE	F171	1977	Vosper T.
AMBUSCADE	F172	1975	Yarrow
ARROW	F173	1976	Yarrow
ALACRITY	F174	1977	Yarrow
ARDENT	F184	1977	Yarrow
AVENGER	F185	1978	Yarrow

Displacement 3,250 tons **Dimensions** 117m x 13m x 6m **Speed** 34 knots **Armament** 1 x 4.5″ gun, 2 x 20mm guns, 4 Exocet Missiles, 1 Sea Cat Missile System, 1 Wasp/Lynx helicopter **Complement** 170.

Notes
Most of the class now have 6 torpedo tubes each.
These General Purpose frigates were built to a commercial design by Vosper/Yarrow and subsequently sold to the Ministry of Defence.

HMS Ashanti

TRIBAL CLASS (Type 81)

Ship	Pennant Number	Completion Date	Builder
ASHANTI	F117	1961	Yarrow
● ESKIMO	F119	1963	White
GURKHA	F122	1963	Thornycroft
ZULU	F124	1964	Stephen
● NUBIAN	F131	1962	HM Dockyard Portsmouth
TARTAR	F133	1962	HM Dockyard Devonport

Displacement 2,700 tons **Dimensions** 110m x 13m x 5m **Speed** 28 knots **Armament** 2 x 4.5" guns, 2 x 20mm guns, 2 Sea Cat Missile Systems, 1 Mortar Mk 10, 1 Wasp helicopter **Complement** 250.

Notes

General Purpose Frigates built for service in the Middle East and West Indies. They were the first ships built to carry a helicopter and have combined steam and gas turbine propulsion. All ships of this class are in the Standby Squadron at Chatham except ASHANTI (see page 112) — and available for sale overseas. ● Approved to Scrap.

HMS Rothesay

ROTHESAY CLASS (Type 12)

Ship	Pennant Number	Completion Date	Builder
YARMOUTH	F101	1960	J. Brown
ROTHESAY	F107	1960	Yarrow
FALMOUTH	F113	1961	Swan Hunter
PLYMOUTH	F126	1961	HM Dockyard Devonport
●RHYL	F129	1960	HM Dockyard Portsmouth

Displacement 2,800 tons **Dimensions** 113m x 13m x 5m
Speed 30 knots **Armament** 2 x 4.5″ guns, 2 x 20mm guns, 1
Sea Cat Missile System, 1 Mortar Mk 10, 1 Wasp helicopter.
Complement 250. ● To Disposal List 1982.

Notes
All ships of this class were follow-on ships to the Whitby Class
and then converted to carry a helicopter.

These ships were the forerunners of the successful Leander
class and have been re-built to Leander standards.

29

HMS Torquay

TYPE 12 (Trials Ships)

Ship	Pennant Number	Completion Date	Builder
TORQUAY	F43	1956	Harland & Wolff
LOWESTOFT	F103	1961	Stephen
LONDONDERRY	F108	1960	J.S. White

Displacement 2,800 tons **Dimensions** 112m x 12m x 5m **Speed** 29 knots **Armament** 2 x 4.5″ guns, 1 Mortar Mk 10. **Complement** 250.

Notes

LOWESTOFT is a sonar trials ship and TORQUAY is used as a Navigational Training ship. LONDONDERRY has been extensively modernised to fit her for her trials role. The ship's weapons systems have been removed and replaced by a computer and new communications and navigation equipment. Equipment under trial can be easily bolted on to the ship: A secondary role is to provide navigation training facilities for young officers.

HMS Ledbury

MINE COUNTERMEASURES SHIPS (MCMV's)
BRECON CLASS

Ship	Pennant Number	Builder
BRECON	M29	Vosper T.
LEDBURY	M30	Vosper T.
CATTISTOCK	M31	Vosper T.
COTTESMORE	M32	Yarrow
BROCKLESBY	M33	Vosper T.
MIDDLETON	M34	Yarrow
DULVERTON	M35	Vosper T.
CHIDDINGFORD	M36	Vosper T.
HURWORTH	M37	Yarrow

Displacement 625 tonnes **Dimensions** 60m x 10m x 2.2m
Speed 17 knots **Armament** 1 x 40mm gun **Complement** 45.

A new class of MCMV being built, albeit in small numbers, to replace the aging Coniston Class over the next few years. The largest Warships ever to be built in Glass Reinforced plastic. Only BRECON & LEDBURY in service — Remainder building. More orders for the RN and overseas sales — to Australia — can be expected.

HMS Kirkliston

CONISTON CLASS

Ship	Pennant Number	Ship	Pennant Number
*ALFRISTON (S)	M1103	HUBBERSTON (H)	M1147
§BICKINGTON (S)	M1109	IVESTON (H)	M1151
BILDESTON (H)	M1110	*KEDLESTON (H)	M1153
*BRERETON (H)	M1113	*KELLINGTON (H)	M1154
BRINTON (H)	M1114	KIRKLISTON (H)	M1157
BRONINGTON (H)	M1115	*LALESTON (S)	M1158
WILTON (H)	M1116	MAXTON (H)	M1165
§CRICHTON (S)	M1124	NURTON (H)	M1166
§CUXTON (S)	M1125	§POLLINGTON (S)	M1173
BOSSINGTON (H)	M1133	§SHAVINGTON (S)	M1180
GAVINTON (H)	M1140	SHERATON (H)	M1181
*HODGESTON (S)	M1146	UPTON (S)	M1187

HMS Shavington

CONISTON CLASS (Cont.)

Ship	Pennant Number	Ship	Pennant Number
§WALKERTON (S)	M1188	§STUBBINGTON(S)	M1204
§WOTTON (S)	M1195	*LEWISTON (S)	M1208
§SOBERTON (S)	M1200	*CROFTON (S)	M1216

Displacement 425 tons **Dimensions** 46m x 9m x 3m **Speed** 15 knots **Armament** 1 x 40mm gun, 2 x 20mm guns **Complement** 29/38.

Notes

120 of this class were built in the early 50s but many have now been sold overseas or scrapped. Have fulfilled many roles over many years and have given excellent service. WILTON, built of glassfibre in 1974, was the world's first 'plastic' warship. Ships marked * are sea training tenders for the RNR. Ships marked § are employed on Coastal Fishery Protection duties. Ships marked (S) are Minesweepers — (H) Minehunters.

HMS St David

Ship	Pennant Number	Completion Date	Builder
ST DAVID	MO7	1972	Cubow
VENTURER	MO8	1973	Cubow

Displacement 392 tonnes **Dimensions** 36m x 9m x 4m
Speed 14 knots. Unarmed. **Complement** 35.

Notes

These two ships are commercial trawlers on charter to the Ministry of Defence. Formerly the Suffolk Harvester (ST DAVID) & Suffolk Monarch. They are equipped for deep team sweeping and operate together as a pair. Both are manned by the RNR.

An order for a class of Minesweepers Medium (MSM's), previously known as EDATS trawlers, has not materialised as expected — they are still "planned". They will replace the current MCMV's manned by the RNR.

HMS Flintham

Ship	Pennant Number	Completion Date	Builder
● AVELEY	M2002	1953	J.S. White
● DITTISHAM	M2621	1954	Fairlie Yacht
● FLINTHAM	M2628	1955	Bolson & Co.
THORNHAM	M2793	1957	Taylor

Displacement 164 tons **Dimensions** 32m x 6m x 2m **Speed** 13 knots **Armament** 1 x 40mm or 20mm gun or unarmed **Complement** 15.

Notes

Sole survivors of the numerically strong 'Ley' and 'Ham' class of inshore minesweepers that still fly the White Ensign. All used for the training of young seamen and RN University Unit personnel. ● To be replaced by 25 metre Fleet Tenders MANLEY, MENTOR and MILLBROOK (and MESSINA?). Future of THORNHAM under review.

HMS Abdiel

MINELAYER
ABDIEL CLASS

Ship	Pennant Number	Completion Date	Builder
ABDIEL	N21	1967	Thornycroft

Displacement 1,500 tons **Dimensions** 80m x 13m x 4m **Speed** 16 knots **Armament** 44 mines 1 x 40mm **Complement** 77.

Notes
Designed as a Headquarters and Support Ship for mine counter measure forces and exercise minelayer. Workshops & spares embarked enable minecountermeasures ships to operate well away from home bases.

ABDIEL is the only operational minelayer in the Royal Navy but plans exist to use merchant ships to lay mines if required. Armed with single 40mm gun during 1981.

HMS Leeds Castle

CASTLE CLASS (OPV2)

Ship	Pennant Number	Completion Date	Builder
LEEDS CASTLE	P258	1981	Hall Russell
DUMBARTON CASTLE	P265	1982	Hall Russell

Displacement 1450 tonnes **Dimensions** 81m x 11m x 3m **Speed** 20 knots **Complement** 40.

Notes

The ships will have a dual role — that of fishery protection and offshore patrols within the limits of UK territorial waters — No less than 270,000 sq. miles! But the OPV2 design is seen by the builders as a multi-purpose vessel with a primary role in offshore protection but with the flexibility to operate as a missile-armed gunboat or anti-submarine corvette — and in a number of civilian applications such as hydrographic research, search and rescue and pollution control. Unlike the Island class these ships are able to operate helicopters.

PATROL VESSELS

HMS Shetland

ISLAND CLASS

Ship	Pennant Number	Completion Date	Builder
ANGLESEY	P277	1979	Hall Russell
ALDERNEY	P278	1979	Hall Russell
JERSEY	P295	1976	Hall Russell
GUERNSEY	P297	1977	Hall Russell
SHETLAND	P298	1977	Hall Russell
ORKNEY	P299	1977	Hall Russell
LINDISFARNE	P300	1978	Hall Russell

Displacement 1,250 tons **Dimensions** 60m x 11m x 4m
Speed 17 knots **Armament** 1 x 40mm gun **Complement** 39.

Notes
Built on trawler lines these ships were introduced to protect the extensive British interests in North Sea oil installations and to patrol the 200 mile fishery limits.

SCIMITAR CLASS

Ship	Pennant Number	Completion Date	Builder
SCIMITAR	P271	1970	Vosper T.
CUTLASS	P274	1970	Vosper T.
SABRE	P275	1970	Vosper T.

Displacement 102 tons **Dimensions** 30m x 8m x 2m **Speed** 40 knots. Unarmed. **Complement** 12.

Notes

These fast training boats were designed to train surface and airborne forces in anti fast patrol boat tactics. They formed the 1st F.T.B. Squadron at Portland but are now in reserve and on the Disposal List (Sales).

HMS Dee

SEAWARD DEFENCE BOATS

Ship	Pennant Number	Completion Date	Builder
DEE	P3104	1953	Wm. Simons
DROXFORD	P3113	1954	Pimblott

Displacement 142 tons **Dimensions** 36m x 6m x 2m **Speed** 18 knots **Complement** 20.

Notes

Designed and built to patrol and defend harbour approaches — equipped with depth charges. Most of the class now scrapped but the above two craft remain as training ships for the RNR and RN University units (at Liverpool and Glasgow).

HMS Wolverton

PATROL BOATS

Ship	Pennant Number	Completion Date	Builder
BEACHAMPTON	P1007	1953	Goole SB
MONKTON	P1055	1956	Herd Mackenzie
WASPERTON	P1089	1956	J.S. White
WOLVERTON	P1093	1957	Montrose SYCo.
YARNTON	P1096	1956	Pickersgill

Displacement 425 tons **Dimensions** 46m x 9m x 3m **Speed** 15 knots **Armament** 2 x 40mm guns **Complement** 32.

Notes
Former Coastal Minesweepers converted to Patrol Boats in 1971 for service in Hong Kong. Conversion involved removal of most minesweeping equipment and fitting extra 40mm gun aft of the funnel. A £40 million order for five replacement vessels has been placed with Hall Russell Ltd of Aberdeen. The new 24 knot steel ships will displace 700 tons. The first will enter service in mid 1983. The Government of Hong Kong will pay 75% of building and maintenance costs of these new ships.

HMS Sandpiper

BIRD CLASS

Ship	Pennant Number	Completion Date	Builder
KINGFISHER	P260	1975	R. Dunston
CYGNET	P261	1976	R. Dunston
PETEREL	P262	1976	R. Dunston
SANDPIPER	P263	1977	R. Dunston

Displacement 190 tons **Dimensions** 37m x 7m x 2m **Speed** 21 knots **Armament** 1 x 40mm gun **Complement** 19.

Notes

Based on the RAF long range recovery vessels, these craft were built for fishery protection .duties. They have not been very successful as they have proved to be bad seaboats. PETEREL and SANDPIPER are now used by Britannia Royal Naval College, Dartmouth, as training ships — the other two ships are employed on coastal patrol duties.

HMS Herald

HECLA CLASS

Ship	Pennant Number	Completion Date	Builder
HECLA	A133	1965	Yarrow
HECATE	A137	1965	Yarrow
HERALD	A138	1974	Robb Caledon
HYDRA	A144	1966	Yarrow

Displacement 2,733 **Dimensions** 79m x 15m x 5m **Speed** 14 knots **Complement** 115.

Notes

Able to operate for long periods away from shore support, these ships and the smaller ships of the Hydrographic Fleet collect the data that is required to produce the Admiralty Charts which are sold to mariners worldwide. Each ship carries a Wasp helicopter. HERALD is an improved version of the earlier ships.

HMS Bulldog

BULLDOG CLASS

Ship	Pennant Number	Completion Date	Builder
BULLDOG	A317	1968	Brooke Marine
BEAGLE	A319	1968	Brooke Marine
FOX	A320	1968	Brooke Marine
FAWN	A335	1968	Brooke Marine

Displacement 1,088 tons **Dimensions** 60m x 11m x 4m **Speed** 15 knots **Complement** 39.

Notes
Designed to operate in coastal waters. All survey ships are painted white and are unarmed. The new class of survey ship planned are similar — but with helicopter facilities.

HMS Egeria

INSHORE SURVEY CRAFT

Ship	Pennant Number	Completion Date	Builder
ECHO	A70	1958	J.S. White
ENTERPRISE	A71	1959	M.W. Blackmore
EGERIA	A72	1959	Wm. Weatherhead
WATERWITCH	M2720	1960	J.S. White
WOODLARK	M2780	1959	J.S. White

Displacement 160 tons **Dimensions** 32m x 7m x 2m **Speed** 14 knots **Complement** 19.

Notes
Built for survey work in harbours, river estuaries, etc. WATER WITCH and WOODLARK were converted from Ham Class inshore minesweepers. They differ slightly from the other ships of the Class and are now used as training ships for University RNR Units. Due to be replaced by an improved class of vessel operating with 15 metre launches and sidewall hovercraft.

HMS Endurance

ICE PATROL SHIP

Ship	Pennant Number	Completion Date	Builder
ENDURANCE (ex MV Anita Dan)	A171	1956	Krogerwerft Rendsburg

Displacement 3,600 tons **Dimensions** 93m x 14m x 5m
Speed 14 knots **Armament** 2 x 20mm guns **Complement** 124.

Notes

Purchased from Denmark in 1967 ENDURANCE is painted brilliant red for easy identification in the ice of Antarctica where she spends 6 months of the year. Her role is to undertake oceanographic and hydrographic surveys in the area and support scientists working ashore. A small Royal Marine detachment is embarked. Two Wasp helicopters are carried for rapid transport of survey personnel & stores. To be "retired early" after her 1982 season in Antarctica.

HMY Britannia

ROYAL YACHT

Ship	Pennant Number	Completion Date	Builder
BRITANNIA	A00	1954	J. Brown

Displacement 4,961 tons **Dimensions** 126m x 17m x 5m
Speed 21 knots. **Complement** 270.

Notes

Probably the best known ship in the Royal Navy, BRITANNIA can quickly be converted to a hospital ship in time of war and is used for NATO exercises when not on 'Royal' business. Dark blue hull and buff funnel. Two extensive refits have brought the ship up to modern-day standards. Normally to be seen in Portsmouth Harbour when not away on official duties.

HMS Speedy

PATROL VESSEL

Ship	Pennant Number	Completion Date	Builder
SPEEDY	P296	1980	Boeing

Displacement 117 tons **Dimensions** 31m x 9m. **Draught** — foilborne 2.4m: Hullborne 5.2m **Speed** 43 knots.

Notes

Purchased 'off the shelf' from Boeing for evaluation as an off-shore patrol vessel — early trials have been successful and excellent availability reported.

HMS Londonderry

HMS Osiris

HMS Hermes

HMS Glamorgan

D19

HMS Birmingham

D86

HM Ships Shetland (top) and Anglesey (bottom)

RFA Gold Rover

RMAS Throsk

HMS Ajax

RFA Tidespring

HMS Active

HMS Wakeful

TUG/SUBMARINE TENDER

Ship	Pennant Number	Builder
WAKEFUL (Ex Dan)	A236	Cochranes
Displacement 900 tons **Dimensions** 39m x 11m x 5m **Speed** 14 knots **Complement** 25.		

Notes
Purchased from Swedish owners in 1974 for duties in the Clyde area as Submarine Target Ship and at the Clyde Submarine Base — HMS NEPTUNE. Has been used for Fishery Protection work and the shadowing of Soviet warships in British waters. Has proved very expensive to keep in service.

HMS Challenger

SEABED OPERATIONS VESSEL

Ship	Pennant Number	Completion Date	Builder
CHALLENGER	K07	Building	Scott Lithgow
Displacement 6,400 tons **Dimensions** 134m x 18m x 5m **Speed** 15 knots **Complement** 185.			

Notes

CHALLENGER will be equipped to find, inspect and, where appropriate, recover objects from the seabed at greater depths than is currently possible. She is designed with a saturation diving system enabling up to 12 men to live in comfort for long periods in a decompression chamber amidships, taking their turns to be lowered in a diving bell to work on the seabed. Also fitted to carry out salvage work. Until CHALLENGER is ready for service the MV SEAFORTH CLANSMAN (3,300 tons) is on charter to the MoD — and operates with an RN diving team.

BH7

HOVERCRAFT

The Royal Naval Hovercraft Trials Unit at Lee-on-Solent is equipped with the following Hovercraft:

3 SRN 6 Craft — For Patrol duties. (2 now in Hong Kong)

1 BH.7 Craft — Trials Craft and MCM support role.

1 VT2 Craft — Support duties for Minecountermeasures forces.

REMEMBER THE GOOD OLD NAVY?

Our series **British Warships since 1945** is proving to be very popular. These books packed with photos (from the famous Wright & Logan Collection) not only give details of all the ships that have served in the RN since World War II but includes a potted history of their careers — and final fate.

PART ONE — covers Battleships, Cruisers, Carriers and Monitors — and is introduced by Admiral Sir Guy Grantham, KCB, CBE, DSO. **£2.20 inc. post**

HMS Bermuda

PART TWO — covers Submarines, Depot & Repair Ships and is introduced by Vice Admiral Sir John Roxburgh, KCB, CBE, DSO, DSC. — a former Flag Officer Submarines. **£2.20 inc. post**

HMS Affray

PART THREE — to be published early in 1982 covers Destroyers — long awaited — £2.95 inc. post

New . . . DEVONPORT BUILT WARSHIPS SINCE 1860
By Lt. Cdr. K.V. Burns, DSM, RN. A superb, illustrated, history of all the ships to be built at this famous yard. Very popular. £2.30 (inc. post).

Send for your copy — by return of post:—
MARITIME BOOKS : DULOE : LISKEARD : CORNWALL PL14 4PE

THE
ROYAL FLEET AUXILIARY

The Royal Fleet Auxiliary Service is operated by the Director of Fuel, Movements and Victualling whose Directorate forms part of the Royal Navy Supply and Transport Service (RNSTS) within the Ministry of Defence (Navy). The RNSTS provides the total logistic support for the Royal Navy and is civilian manned throughout under the management of the Director General of Supplies and Transport (Navy).

All Royal Fleet Auxiliaries are manned by Merchant Navy personnel and operate under their own distinctive flag — a blue ensign with a vertical anchor in gold in the fly, which distinguishes them from other non commissioned ships and craft engaged in the Naval Service. All officers and some 40-50% of ratings serve under contract to the Royal Fleet Auxiliary Service.

The RFA Fleet currently comprises 5 large fleet tankers (OL and TIDE Classes), 5 smaller fleet tankers (ROVER Class), 4 Support tankers (LEAF Class), 5 Store Support ships (one NESS Class, REGENT, RESOURCE and two FORT Class), RFA ENGADINE (helicopter support ship) and 6 Landing Ships (Logistic) supporting the British Army of the Rhine (LANCELOT Class).

As a result of the Government's commitment to reduce public expenditure, Defence, with its substantial budget, has had to bear its share of such a reduction, and in turn the RFA Service has had to make its contribution.

RFA EDDYFIRTH (Coastal tanker) was withdrawn from service in April 81 and the long term charter of RFA BACCHUS (Cargo freighter) came to an end in November 81 when she was handed back to her owners, their tasks being absorbed without replacement.

In addition, the 1981 Defence review has resulted in the withdrawal from service of three front line RFAs by the end of 1983 — RFAs TIDEPOOL and TIDESPRING (Fleet tankers) and RFA STROMNESS (Stores Support Ship).

However, the RFA future remains bright and the afloat support role of the service continues to grow placing new demands on its officers and ratings and calling for greater operational sophistication and flexibility. A third new support tanker, RFA BAYLEAF, will join the Fleet in April 1982, and the future will also see the advent of a newer and more versatile RFA — combining features which are now present in separate vessels all in one hull.

Although the primary role of the RFA Service remains the

underway replenishment of fuel, stores, ammunition and food to the Fleet, the frequent embarkation of Sea King helicopters in front line RFAs gives many an RFA an anti-submarine training role in support of the Royal Navy. This role has added an extra dimension calling for new skills in seamanship and flight deck operations onboard. The Service remains ready to live up to what it has always proclaimed itself to be — "Ready for Anything".

It will be interesting to see if ships of the RFA will be used to take more and more RN personnel to sea for basic training now that the number of ships in the RN is being reduced — and the Defence review promises more training to be carried out at sea.

Finally, readers associated with the work of the RFA will be aware of the close connection which the RFA maintains with its US Navy 'Sister Service' — the Military Sealift Command (MSC). During the last couple of years a considerable exchange of views has taken place which lead to an agreement to release RFAs LYNESS and TARBATNESS to the Military Sealift Command. Both ships have since been formally handed over to the MSC at Norfolk, Virginia and renamed SIRIUS and SPICA respectively. This transfer of RFA LYNESS and TARBATNESS has created a visible symbol of the very close ties which have developed over the years between two organisations which share common objectives.

SHIPS OF THE ROYAL FLEET AUXILIARY
Pennant Numbers

Ship	Penn. No.	Ship	Penn. No.
TIDESPRING	A75	BLACK ROVER	A273
TIDEPOOL	A76	STROMNESS	A344
PEARLEAF	A77	FORT GRANGE	A385
PLUMLEAF	A78	FORT AUSTIN	A386
APPLELEAF	A79	RESOURCE	A480
BRAMBLELEAF	A81	REGENT	A486
BAYLEAF		ENGADINE	K08
OLWEN	A122	SIR BEDIVERE	L3004
OLNA	A123	SIR GALAHAD	L3005
OLMEDA	A124	SIR GERAINT	L3027
GREEN ROVER	A268	SIR LANCELOT	L3029
GREY ROVER	A269	SIR PERCIVAL	L3036
BLUE ROVER	A270	SIR TRISTRAM	L3505
GOLD ROVER	A271		

RFA Olmeda

'OL' CLASS

Ship	Pennant Number	Completion Date	Builder
OLWEN	A122	1965	Hawthorn Leslie
OLNA	A123	1966	Hawthorn Leslie
OLMEDA	A124	1965	Swan Hunter

Displacement 36,000 tons **Dimensions** 197m x 26m x 10m
Speed 19 knots **Complement** 94.

Notes
These ships can carry up to 3 Wessex helicopters. Dry stores can be carried — and transferred at sea — as well as a wide range of fuel, aviation spirit and lubricants.

T
A
N
K
E
R
S

63

RFA Tidespring

TIDE CLASS

Ship	Pennant Number	Completion Date	Builder
TIDESPRING	A75	1963	Hawthorn Leslie
TIDEPOOL	A76	1963	Hawthorn Leslie

Displacement 27,400 tons **Dimensions** 177m x 22m x 10m
Speed 18 knots **Complement** 110.

Notes
Built to fuel warships at sea in any part of the world including strengthening for ice operations. A hangar and flight deck provides space for three Wessex helicopters if required. Both ships to be "retired early" during 1982/3.

RFA Blue Rover

ROVER CLASS

Ship	Pennant Number	Completion Date	Builder
GREEN ROVER	A268	1969	Swan Hunter
GREY ROVER	A269	1970	Swan Hunter
BLUE ROVER	A270	1970	Swan Hunter
GOLD ROVER	A271	1974	Swan Hunter
BLACK ROVER	A273	1974	Swan Hunter

Displacement 11,522 tons **Dimensions** 141m x 19m x 7m
Speed 18 knots **Complement** 50.

Notes
Small Fleet Tankers designed to supply HM ships with fresh water, dry cargo and refrigerated provisions as well as a range of fuel and lubricants. Due to initial engineering problems some of the class have had to be re-engined.

RFA Appleleaf

LEAF CLASS [New]

Ship	Pennant Number	Completion Date	Builder
APPLELEAF	A79	1980	Cammell Laird
BRAMBLE-LEAF	A81	1980	Cammell Laird

Displacement 20,434 tonnes **Dimensions** 170m x 26m x 12m
Speed 14.5 knots **Complement** 60.

Notes

Both are ex Merchant Vessels (Hudson Deep & Hudson Cavelier) taken over by the Ministry when part completed. A new (30,000 ton) ship is being built by Cammell Laird for charter to MoD — to be named BAYLEAF.

RFA Plumleaf

LEAF CLASS [Old]

Ship	Pennant Number	Completion Date	Builder
PEARLEAF	A77	1960	Blythwood
PLUMLEAF	A78	1960	Blyth D.D.

Displacement Both about 25,000 tons **Dimensions** 170m x 22m x 7m **Speed** 15 knots **Complement** 55.

Notes

These 2 different ships are on long term charter to the Ministry of Defence from their civilian owners and are employed on freighting duties between oil terminals, but have limited replenishment facilities to fuel HM ships at sea. One ship will be retired when BAYLEAF enters service.

RFA Fort Grange

FORT CLASS

Ship	Pennant Number	Completion Date	Builder
FORT GRANGE	A385	1978	Scott Lithgow
FORT AUSTIN	A386	1979	Scott Lithgow

Displacement 17,000 tons **Dimensions** 183m x 24m x 9m
Speed 20 knots **Complement** 133.

Notes

These ships can carry a wide range of armament stores, ammunition, naval stores, dry and refrigerated provisions and NAAFI stores for supply to warships at sea.

Full hangar and maintenance facilities are provided and up to four Sea King helicopters can be carried for both the transfer of stores and anti-submarine protection of a group of ships.

RFA Stromness

NESS CLASS

Ship	Pennant Number	Completion Date	Builder
STROMNESS	A344	1967	Swan Hunter

Displacement 16,500 tons **Dimensions** 160m x 22m x 7m **Speed** 17 knots **Complement** 105.

Notes

LYNESS was deleted from the RFA Fleet in 1980 and TARBAT-NESS in 1981 — both are now in service with US Navy (Military Sealift Command). STROMNESS to be "retired early" in 1982 — and could follow sister ships to USA.

RFA Resource

REGENT CLASS

Ship	Pennant Number	Completion Date	Builder
RESOURCE	A480	1967	Scotts
REGENT	A486	1967	Harland & Wolff
Displacement 22,890 tons **Dimensions** 195m x 24m x 8m **Speed** 21 knots **Complement** 123.			

Notes

The only RFA ships with an RN helicopter permanently embarked for supplying ships with a full range of the Naval Armament stores and ammunition carried aboard. A limited range of Naval Stores and food is also carried.

RFA Sir Lancelot

LANDING SHIPS
SIR LANCELOT CLASS   ING SHIPS

Ship	Pennant Number	Completion Date	Builder
SIR BEDIVERE	L3004	1967	Hawthorn
SIR GALAHAD	L3005	1966	Stephen
SIR GERAINT	L3027	1967	Stephen
SIR LANCELOT	L3029	1964	Fairfield
SIR PERCIVAL	L3036	1968	Hawthorn
SIR TRISTRAM	L3505	1967	Hawthorn

Displacement 5,550 tons **Dimensions** 126m x 18m x 4m **Speed** 17 knots **Armament** Can be fitted with 2 x 40mm guns in emergency **Complement** 69.

Notes

Manned by the RFA but tasked by the Army, these ships are used for heavy transport of stores — embarked by bow and stern doors — and beach assault landings. Can operate helicopters from tank deck if required.

RFA Engadine

RFA ENGADINE

Ship	Pennant Number	Completion Date	Builder
ENGADINE	K08	1967	Robb
Displacement 9,000 tons **Dimensions** 129m x 17m x 7m **Speed** 16 knots **Complement** 73 (+ RN group).			

Notes
Specially built for RFA service (but with embarked RN personnel) to provide training ship for helicopter crews operating in deep waters well away from coasts. Can operate up to 6 helicopters and often embarks pilotless target aircraft for exercises. Hangar for them above main hangar.

ROYAL MARITIME AUXILIARY SERVICE

The Royal Maritime Auxiliary Service fleet, comprising approximately 700 hulls, over 400 of which are self-propelled, is one of the largest marine undertakings in the country. It is administered by the Director of Marine Service (Naval), to whom the Captains of the Ports and Resident Naval Officers at the various Naval Bases are mainly responsible for the provision of Marine Services for the Royal Navy and other Ministry of Defence authorities.

Ships of the RMAS, which can be seen at work in any of the Naval Bases throughout the United Kingdom, are easily identified by their black hulls and buff coloured superstructure and funnels, and by the RMAS flag, which is a blue ensign defaced in the fly by a yellow anchor over two wavy lines. The pennant numbers of the larger ships are painted in white on their black hulls.

The largest section of the fleet is employed on harbour duties, the types of vessel involved being Harbour Tugs, Fleet Tenders, Tank Cleaning Vessels, Degaussing Vessels, Harbour Launches, Naval Armament Vessels and Dumb Lighters for carrying ammunition, general stores, oil, water and victuals to the Royal Navy, NATO Navies and Royal Fleet Auxiliary Ships when they are in port or at anchor.

A smaller section of the RMAS is, however, engaged in a purely sea-going capacity. Ocean-going tugs, Torpedo Recovery Vessels and Mooring and Salvage Vessels are designed and equipped for world-wide towing and complex Marine Salvage operations. Experimental Trials Vessels, fitted with some of the most modern sophisticated equipment, are deployed on a wide range of duties in the fast-growing area of advanced experimental technology necessary for the design of new ships, weapons and machinery.

Oil pollution is becoming more prevalent, and to deal with emergencies which may arise around the coastline of the United Kingdom, the RMAS has adapted many of its vessels to contain dispersant chemicals and to fit spraying equipment as a prerequisite to assisting the Department of Trade in combating oil pollution in waters outside Dockyard Ports.

At the time of writing, the implications of the 1981 Defence Review have not been felt by the RMAS. With the complete closure of the Chatham yard and a smaller Portsmouth base, a reduction in the size of the RMAS fleet must be expected in the longer term. With the current RMAS fleet being the most modern it has ever been, it will be difficult to see where the axe should fall.

Readers of this book will doubtless note that for the size of the front line RN fleet, the size of the RMAS can only be described as massive. It cannot be long before some new cost-cutting review committee will take a close look at the RMAS to see if these ships can either be given secondary rôles or some of their tasks be undertaken by civilian vessels on charter.

Undoubtedly the RMAS has given, and will continue to give, the RN excellent back-up services — whether the "new look" Navy can afford it — only time will tell.

SHIPS OF THE ROYAL MARITIME AUXILIARY SERVICE — PENNANT NUMBERS

Ship	Penn. No.	Ship	Penn. No.
MELTON	A83	BEMBRIDGE	A101
MENAI	A84	AIREDALE	A102
MEON	A87	BIBURY	A103
AGILE	A88	BLAKENEY	A104
ADVICE	A89	BRODICK	A105
ACCORD	A90		
MILFORD	A91	ALSATIAN	A106
TYPHOON	A95	CYCLONE	A111
BEAULIEU	A99	FELICITY	A112
BEDDGELERT	A100	ALICE	A113

Ship	Penn. No.	Ship	Penn. No.
MAGNET	A114	IRENE	A181
LODESTONE	A115	SALUKI	A182
AGATHA	A116	ISABEL	A183
AUDREY	A117	POINTER	A188
AGNES	A121	SETTER	A189
CAIRN	A126	JOAN	A190
TORRID	A127	JOYCE	A193
TORRENT	A128	GWENDOLINE	A196
DALMATIAN	A129	SEALYHAM	A197
TORNADO	A140	HELEN	A198
TORCH	A141	MYRTLE	A199
TORMENTOR	A142	SPANIEL	A201
TOREADOR	A143	NANCY	A202
DAISY	A145	NORAH	A205
WATERMAN	A146	LLANDOVERY	A207
FRANCES	A147	LAMLASH	A208
FIONA	A148	CHARLOTTE	A210
FLORENCE	A149	LECHLADE	A211
GENEVIEVE	A150	ENDEAVOUR	A213
GEORGINA	A152	BEE	A216
DEERHOUND	A155	CHRISTINE	A217
DAPHNE	A156	CLARE	A218
LOYAL HELPER	A157	LOYAL	
SUPPORTER	A158	MODERATOR	A220
LOYAL WATCHER	A159	ADEPT	A224
LOYAL VOLUNTEER	A160	BUSTLER	A225
LOYAL MEDIATOR	A161	CAPABLE	A226
ELKHOUND	A162	CAREFUL	A227
GOOSANDER	A164	CRICKET	A229
POCHARD	A165	COCKCHAFER	A230
KATHLEEN	A166	KINGARTH	A232
LABRADOR	A168	GNAT	A239
KITTY	A170	SHEEPDOG	A250
LESLEY	A172	DORIS	A252
DOROTHY	A173	LADYBIRD	A253
LILAH	A174	CICALA	A263
MARY	A175	SCARAB	A272
EDITH	A177	ETTRICK	A274
HUSKY	A178	ELSING	A277
MASTIFF	A180	KINBRACE	A281

Ship	Penn. No.	Ship	Penn. No.
AURICULA	A285	CROMARTY	A488
CONFIANCE	A289	DORNOCH	A490
CONFIDENT	A290	ROLLICKER	A502
ILCHESTER	A308	UPLIFTER	A507
INSTOW	A309	HEADCORN	A1766
IRONBRIDGE	A311	HEVER	A1767
IXWORTH	A318	HARLECH	A1768
BETTY	A322	HAMBLEDON	A1769
BRIDGET	A323	LOYAL	
BARBARA	A324	CHANCELLOR	A1770
BRENDA	A325	LOYAL PROCTOR	A1771
FOXHOUND	A326	HOLMWOOD	A1772
BASSET	A327	HORNING	A1773
COLLIE	A328	PAGHAM	M2716
CORGI	A330	WATERWITCH	M2720
FOTHERBY	A341	SHIPHAM	M2726
FELSTEAD	A348	PORTISHAM	M2781
CARTMEL	A350	THATCHAM	M2790
CAWSAND	A351	SANDRINGHAM	M2791
ELKSTONE	A353	MANDARIN	P192
FROXFIELD	A354	PINTAIL	P193
EPWORTH	A355	GARGANEY	P194
DATCHET	A357	GOLDENEYE	P195
ROYSTERER	A361	ABERDOVEY	Y10
DENMEAD	A363	ABINGER	Y11
WHITEHEAD	A364	ALNESS	Y12
FULBECK	A365	ALNMOUTH	Y13
ROBUST	A366	ASHCOTT	Y16
NEWTON	A367	WATERFALL	Y17
KINTERBURY	A378	WATERSHED	Y18
THROSK	A379	WATERSPOUT	Y19
CRICKLADE	A381	WATERSIDE	Y20
APPLEBY	A383	OILPRESS	Y21
CLOVELLY	A389	OILSTONE	Y22
CRICCIETH	A391	OILWELL	Y23
GLENCOE	A392	OILFIELD	Y24
DUNSTER	A393	OILBIRD	Y25
FINTRY	A394	OILMAN	Y26
GRASMERE	A402	WATERCOURSE	Y30
KINLOSS	A482	WATERFOWL	Y31

RMAS Rollicker

ROYSTERER CLASS

Ship	Pennant Number	Completion Date	Builder
ROYSTERER	A361	1972	C.D. Holmes
ROBUST	A366	1974	C.D. Holmes
ROLLICKER	A502	1973	C.D. Holmes

G.R.T. 1036 tons **Dimensions** 54m x 12m x 6m
Speed 15 knots **Complement** 31.

Notes
Built for salvage and long range towage, but are also used for harbour duties.

RMAS Typhoon

TYPHOON CLASS

Ship	Pennant Number	Completion Date	Builder
TYPHOON	A95	1960	Henry Robb

G.R.T. 1034 tons	**Dimensions** 60m x 12m x 4m	
Speed 17 knots	**Complement** 80.	

Long range towage and salvage tug. Now based at Portland and employed mainly on target towing and trials work. One older 'Bustler' class tug remains in service — CYCLONE (A111) — and is based at Gibraltar.

RMAS Agile

CONFIANCE CLASS

Ship	Pennant Number	Completion Date	Builder
AGILE	A88	1959	Goole SB Co.
ADVICE	A89	1959	A & J Inglis
ACCORD	A90	1958	A & J Inglis
CONFIANCE	A289	1956	A & J Inglis
CONFIDENT	A290	1956	A & J Inglis

Displacement 760 tons **Dimensions** 47m x 11m x 4m **Speed** 13 knots **Complement** 29.

Notes
Minor differences exist between the last two ships of the class.
Employed in harbour, coastal towage and target towing duties.
AGILE — now based at Gibraltar.

79

RMAS Adept

HARBOUR TUGS
TWIN UNIT TRACTOR TUGS (TUTT'S)

Ship	Pennant Number	Completion Date	Builder
ADEPT	A224	1981	R. Dunston
BUSTLER	A225	1981	R. Dunston
CAPABLE	A226	1982	R. Dunston
CAREFUL	A227	1982	R. Dunston
G.R.T. 375 tons	**Dimensions** 39m x 10m x 4m		
Speed 12 knots	**Complement** 9		

A new class of tug built to replace the Confiance Class and paddletugs of the Director Class — all now retired.

DOG CLASS

Ship	Pennant Number	Ship	Pennant Number
AIREDALE	A102	POINTER	A188
ALSATIAN	A106	SETTER	A189
CAIRN	A126	SEALYHAM	A197
DALMATIAN	A129	SPANIEL	A201
DEERHOUND	A155	SHEEPDOG	A250
ELKHOUND	A162	FOXHOUND	A326
LABRADOR	A168	BASSET	A327
HUSKY	A178	COLLIE	A328
MASTIFF	A180	CORGIE	A330
SALUKI	A182		

GRT 152 tons **Dimensions** 29m x 8m x 4m **Speed** 12 knots **Complement** 8.

Notes

General harbour tugs — all completed between 1962 & 1972.

RMAS Clare

IMPROVED GIRL CLASS

Ship	Pennant Number	Ship	Pennant Number
DAISY	A145	CHARLOTTE	A210
DAPHNE	A156	CHRISTINE	A217
DOROTHY	A173	CLARE	A218
EDITH	A177	DORIS	A252
G.R.T. 75 tons **Speed** 10 knots **Complement** 6.			

Notes
All completed 1971-2. CLARE is now serving in RN colours and with an RN crew on anti-illegal immigrant patrols in Hong Kong waters.

IRENE CLASS

Ship	Pennant Number	Ship	Pennant Number
KATHLEEN	A166	ISABEL	A183
KITTY	A170	JOAN	A190
LESLEY	A172	JOYCE	A193
LILAH	A174	MYRTLE	A199
MARY	A175	NANCY	A202
IRENE	A181	NORAH	A205

G.R.T. 89 tons **Speed** 8 knots **Complement** 6.

Notes
Known as Water Tractors these craft are used for basin moves and towage of light barges.

RMAS Frances

FELICITY CLASS

Ship	Pennant Number	Ship	Pennant Number
FELICITY	A112	GENEVIEVE	A150
FRANCES	A147	GEORGINA	A152
FIONA	A148	GWENDOLINE	A196
FLORENCE	A149	HELEN	A198
G.R.T. 80 tons **Speed** 10 knots **Complement** 6.			

Notes

Water Tractors — completed in 1973: FRANCES,
FLORENCE & GENEVIEVE completed 1980.

RMAS Bridget

GIRL CLASS

Ship	Pennant Number	Ship	Pennant Number
ALICE	A113	BETTY	A322
AGATHA	A116	BRIDGET	A323
AUDREY	A117	BARBARA	A324
AGNES	A121	BRENDA	A325

G.R.T. 38 tons **Speed** 10 knots **Complement** 6.

Notes
Completed 1962-1972. General duties light tugs.

TRIALS SHIPS

Ship	Pennant Number	Completion Date	Builder
WHITEHEAD	A364	1971	Scotts

G.R.T. 3427 tons **Dimensions** 97m x 15m x 5m **Speed** 15.5 knots **Complement** 57.

Notes
Fitted with Torpedo Tubes for trial firings.

RMAS Newton

Ship	Pennant Number	Completion Date	Builder
NEWTON	A367	1976	Scotts
G.R.T. 2779 tons **Dimensions** 99m x 16m x 6m **Speed** 15 knots **Complement** 64			

Notes

Built as sonar propagation trials ships but can also be used as Cable Layer.

RMAS Auricula

TEST & EXPERIMENTAL SONAR TENDER

Ship	Pennant Number	Completion Date	Builder
AURICULA	A285	1981	Ferguson Bros

G.R.T. 981 tons	**Dimensions** 52m x 11m x 3m
Speed 12 knots	**Complement** 18

RMAS Kinterbury

ARMAMENT STORES CARRIERS

Ship	Pennant Number	Completion Date	Builder
KINTERBURY	A378	1980	Appledore S B
THROSK	A379	1977	Cleland SB Co.

G.R.T. 1357 tons. **Dimensions** 64m x 12m x 5m
Speed 14 knots **Complement** 22.

Notes
2 holds carry Naval armament stores, ammunition and guided missiles. Employed on short coastal journeys between Naval Bases. Kinterbury varies slightly from earlier sister ship.

RMAS Cricket

INSECT CLASS

Ship	Pennant Number	Completion Date	Builder
BEE	A216	1970	C.D. Holmes
CRICKET	A229	1972	Beverley
COCKCHAFER	A230	1971	Beverley
GNAT	A239	1972	Beverley
LADYBIRD	A253	1973	Beverley
CICALA	A263	1971	Beverley
SCARAB	A272	1973	Beverley

G.R.T. 279 tons **Dimensions** 34m x 8m x 3m **Speed** 10.5 knots **Complement** 10.

Notes

3 completed as Stores Carriers, 3 as Armament Stores Carriers and SCARAB is fitted as a Mooring Vessel.

RNXS Loyal Watcher

LOYAL CLASS

Ship	Penn No.	Ship	Penn No.
LOYAL HELPER	A157	LOYAL MEDIATOR	A161
SUPPORTER	A158	LOYAL MODERATOR	A220
LOYAL WATCHER	A159	LOYAL CHANCELLOR	A1770
LOYAL VOLUNTEER	A160	LOYAL PROCTOR	A1771

G.R.T. 112 tons **Dimensions** 24m x 6m x 3m **Speed** 10.5 knots **Complement** 6.

Notes

All these craft are operated by the Royal Naval Auxiliary Service (RNXS) — men (and women) — who in time of emergency would man these craft for duties as port control vessels. HMS ALERT and VIGILANT are similar and were taken over from the RNXS. PORTISHAM and SHIPHAM (ex I.M.S's) are still in service with the RNXS.

T
E
N
D
E
R
S

RMAS Epworth

CLOVELLY CLASS

Ship	Penn. No.	Ship	Penn. No.
MELTON	A83	DENMEAD	A363
MENAI	A84	CRICKLADE	A381
MEON	A87	CLOVELLY	A389
MILFORD	A91	CRICCIETH	A391
LLANDOVERY	A207	GLENCOE	A392
LAMLASH	A208	DUNSTER	A393
LECHLADE	A211	FINTRY	A394
ETTRICK	A274	GRASMERE	A402
ELSING	A277	CROMARTY	A488
ILCHESTER*	A308	DORNOCH	A490
INSTOW*	A309	HEADCORN	A1766
IRONBRIDGE*	A311	HEVER	A1767
IXWORTH*	A318	HARLECH	A1768
FOTHERBY	A341	HAMBLEDON	A1769
FELSTEAD	A348	HOLMWOOD	A1772
ELKSTONE	A353	HORNING	A1773
FROXFIELD	A354		
EPWORTH	A355	DATCHET	A357

G.R.T. 78 tons   **Dimensions** 24m x 6m x 3m
Speed 10.5 knots   **Complement** 6

Notes
All completed since 1971 to replace Motor Fishing Vessels. Vessels marked * are diving tenders. Remainder are Training Tenders, Passenger Ferries, or Cargo Vessels. DATCHET (A357) is a diving tender — not of this class but similar.

RMAS Cartmel

ABERDOVEY CLASS

Ship	Pennant Number	Ship	Pennant Number
ABERDOVEY	Y10	BEAULIEU	A99
ABINGER	Y11	BEDDGELERT	A100
ALNESS	Y12	BEMBRIDGE	A101
ALNMOUTH	Y13	BIBURY	A103
ASHCOTT	Y16	BLAKENEY	A104
APPLEBY	A383	BRODICK	A105
CARTMEL	A350	CAWSAND	A351

G.R.T. 77 tons **Dimensions** 24m x 5m x 3m **Speed** 10.5 knots **Complement** 6.

Notes

ALNMOUTH is a Sea Cadet Training Ship based at Plymouth, BEMBRIDGE has similiar duties at Portsmouth.

RMAS Thatcham

INSHORE CRAFT

Ship	Penn. No.	Ship	Penn. No.
PAGHAM ★	M2716	THATCHAM ★	M2790
SHIPHAM ●	M2726	SANDRINGHAM	M2791
PORTISHAM ●	M2781		

Displacement 164 tons   **Dimensions** 32m x 6m x 2m
Speed 12 knots   **Complement** c15

Notes

All are ex Inshore Minesweepers (see page 35) converted for
alternative roles. Vessels marked ● are training ships for the
RNXS and those marked ★ were converted for RMAS/RNXS
service but are now used as RNR training ships. SANDRING-
HAM is used as a Clyde ferry for service personnel.

RMAS Oilman

OILPRESS CLASS

Ship	Pennant Number	Completion Date	Builder
OILPRESS	Y21	1969	Appledore Shipbuilders
OILSTONE	Y22	1969	" "
OILWELL	Y23	1969	" "
OIL FIELD	Y24	1969	" "
OILBIRD	Y25	1969	" "
OILMAN	Y26	1969	" "

G.R.T. 362 tons **Dimensions** 41m x 9m x 3m **Speed** 11 knots **Complement** 11.

Notes
Employed as Harbour and Coastal Oilers.

RMAS Waterside

WATER CARRIERS
WATER CLASS

Ship	Pennant Number	Completion Date	Builder
WATERCOURSE	Y15	1974	Drypool Eng. Co.
WATERFOWL	Y16	1974	Drypool Eng. Co.
WATERFALL	Y17	1967	Drypool Eng. Co.
WATERSHED	Y18	1967	Drypool Eng. Co.
WATERSPOUT	Y19	1967	Drypool Eng. Co.
WATERSIDE	Y20	1968	Drypool Eng. Co.
WATERMAN	A146	1978	Drypool Eng. Co.

G.R.T. 263 tons **Dimensions** 40m x 8m x 2m **Speed** 11 knots **Complement** 11.

Notes
Capable of coastal passages, these craft normally supply either demineralised or fresh water to the Fleet within port limits.

RMAS Lodestone

DEGAUSSING VESSELS
MAGNET CLASS

Ship	Pennant Number	Completion Date	Builder
MAGNET	A114	1979	Cleland
LODESTONE	A115	1980	Cleland

G.R.T. 828 tons **Dimensions** 55m x 12m x 4m
Speed 14 knots

Notes.
A new class of vessel to replace those Ham Class minesweepers converted for D.G. work.

RMAS Torrent

TORPEDO RECOVERY VESSELS (TRV's)
TORRID CLASS

Ship	Pennant Number	Completion Date	Builder
TORRID	A127	1971	Cleland SB Co.
TORRENT	A128	1972	Cleland SB Co.

G.R.T. 550 tons **Dimensions** 46m x 9m x 3m **Speed** 12 knots **Complement** 17.

Notes
A stern ramps is built for the recovery of torpedoes fired for trials and exercises. A total of 32 can be carried.

RMAS Toreador

TORNADO CLASS

Ship	Pennant Number	Completion Date	Builder
TORNADO	A140	1979	Hall Russell
TORCH	A141	1980	Hall Russell
TORMENTOR	A142	1980	Hall Russell
TOREADOR	A143	1980	Hall Russell

G.R.T. 560 tons **Dimensions** 47m x 8m x 3m
Speed 14 knots **Complement** 17.

Notes
Have now replaced the 6 former inshore minesweepers converted for torpedo recovery work — all are now for sale.

T
R
V's

RMAS St Margarets

Ship	Pennant Number	Completion Date	Builder
ST MARGARETS	A259	1944	Swan Hunter
Displacement 1,300 tons **Dimensions** 76m x 11m x 5m **Speed** 12 knots			

Last true cable ship in Naval service — but also employed on trials duties. Sole survivor of triple expansion steam propulsion in the fleet.

RMAS Mandarin

WILD DUCK CLASS

Ship	Pennant Number	Completion Date	Builder
MANDARIN	P192	1964	C. Laird
PINTAIL	P193	1964	C. Laird
GARGANEY	P194	1966	Brooke Marine
GOLDENEYE	P195	1966	Brooke Marine
GOOSANDER	A164	1973	Robb Caledon
POCHARD	A165	1973	Robb Caledon

G.R.T. 900 tons * **Dimensions** 58m x 12m x 4m
Speed 10 knots **Complement** 26.
* Vessels vary slightly.

Notes
Vessels capable of carrying out a wide range of duties laying moorings and boom defences and heavy lift salvage work. 50 tons can be lifted over the horns and 200 tons over the bow.

RMAS Kinloss

KIN CLASS

Ship	Pennant Number	Completion Date	Builder
KINGARTH	A232	1945	A. Hall Aberdeen
KINBRACE	A281	1944	A. Hall Aberdeen
KINLOSS	A482	1945	A. Hall Aberdeen
UPLIFTER	A507	1944	Smith's Dock

Displacement 1,050 tons **Dimensions** 54m x 11m x 4m **Speed** 9 knots **Complement** 34.

Notes
Coastal Salvage Vessels re-engined between 1963 & 1967. Now have same role as Wild Duck Class. LAYMOOR (P190) ex RN manned — in reserve at Gibraltar.

RMAS Dolwen

DOLWEN CLASS

Ship	Pennant Number	Completion Date	Builder
DOLWEN (ex Hector Gulf)		1962	P.K. Harris
Displacement 602 tons **Dimensions** 41m x 9m x 4m **Speed** 14 knots.			

Notes
Built as a stern trawler, then purchased for use as a Buoy tender — now used as Safety Vessel for RAE ABERPORTH (S. Wales). ENDEAVOUR is a Torpedo Recovery/Trials Vessel at Portland.

The Fleet Air Arm

AIRCRAFT OF THE FLEET AIR ARM . . .

British Aerospace — SEA HARRIER FRS Mk 1

VSTOL. The Sea Harrier is a maritime strike/fighter/reconnaissance aircraft now in service in HM ships Invincible and Hermes.

Crew one   **Length** 47′   **Height** 12′   **Wing Span** 25′   **Speed** 650 knots +.

Powered by one Rolls Royce vectored thrust Pegasus turbo jet. 34 are on order.

Scottish Aviation Jetstream

The 'flying classroom' for Fleet Air Arm Observers. Based at RNAS Culdrose, Cornwall. 14 in service and 2 more on order.

Crew 1/2 (Plus instructor and two students)   **Length** 48′   **Height** 18′   **Wing Span** 52′   **Speed** 215 knots.

Westland SEA KING

Anti-submarine helicopter fitted with advance avionics including dipping sonar and radar. Armed with torpedoes and depth charges. Able to operate in all weathers and at night. 69 are in service. **Crew** Four **Length** 72′ **Height** 17′ **Rotor Diameter** 62′ **Speed** 125 knots. Can be used for "heavy lift" sorties. Powered by two Rolls Royce Gnome engines.

17 new SEA KING MK V are in service. Equipped with Sonobuoys as well as sonar. They greatly improve submarine hunting capabilities. Older Mk I and Mk II aircraft are being updated to Mk V specification.

Westland LYNX

Anti-submarine attack, surface search and strike helicopter. Replacing the Wasp in small ships of the fleet. 60 delivered and a further 20 Mk 3 versions on order. Can be armed with 2 homing torpedoes, depth charges or missiles. **Crew** Two **Length** 49′ **Height** 11′ **Rotor Diameter** 42′ **Speed** 150 knots.
Powered by two Rolls Royce Gem turboshaft engines.

Westland SEA KING Mk 4

A close derivative of the anti-submarine Sea King. Able to lift 8,000 lbs — more than twice the capability of the Wessex and to transport 27 fully equipped Royal Marine Commandos. 15 are on order. **Crew** Three **Length** 56′ **Height** 16′ **Rotor Diameter** 62′ **Speed** 140 knots.
Powered by two Rolls Royce Gnome (uprated) engines.

Westland WESSEX Mk 5

Similar to the Mk 3, this aircraft is primarily used for troop carrying duties. Bulky loads, including Land Rovers, can be carried as underslung loads. Can carry air-to-air missiles and, in emergency, can be used as a torpedo launching aircraft. All Search and Rescue aircraft are now Wessex V's.

Length 65′ **Height** 16′ **Rotor Diameter** 56′ **Speed** 115 knots.

Powered by two Rolls Royce Bristol Gnome engines.

Westland WASP

Anti-submarine and F.P.B. helicopter carried by frigates. Armed with 2 torpedoes or missiles. Also carried for general duties in H Class Survey Ships and HMS ENDURANCE. Being replaced by the Lynx, but are expected to remain in service (in small numbers) until 1992.

Crew 1/2 **Length** 40′ **Height** 11′ **Rotor Diameter** 32′ **Speed** 110 knots.

Powered by one Rolls Royce Nimbus turboshaft engine.

Westland WESSEX Mk 3

Anti-submarine aircraft carried by County Class Destroyers — predecessor of the Sea King. The large hump behind the rotor head houses the radar scanner. Will disappear from service shortly.

Details as for the Wessex Mk 5.

Westland / Aerospatiale GAZELLE

Helicopter Trainer. Joint French/UK aircraft used for pilot training and spotter duties by the Royal Marines. A variety of armaments can be carried. **Crew** one **Length** 39′ **Height** 10′. **Rotor Diameter** 34′ **Speed** 167 knots.
Powered by one Turbomeca Astazon 111A turboshaft engine. 28 in service.

For the full story you'll want to read

Flashing Blades over the Sea
By Lt. Cdr. J. M. Milne, RN

The complete history of the helicopter in the Royal Navy — since 1943. Written by a serving Fleet Air Arm officer — and introduced by HRH The Prince of Wales. 104 pages. Over 80 photographs. 8 pages in full colour.

£2.10 (including postage)

From Maritime Books, Duloe, Liskeard PL14 4PE.

Communications Aircraft

With the disbandment of 781 Squadron at Lee-on-Solent last year, 6 Sea Devons are now for sale. RNAS Culdrose and Yeovilton have 3 aircraft each for Fishing Protection duties and other general flying duties.

Sea Heron C Mk 1 [top]
Crew 2/3 **Length** 48′ **Height** 16′ **Wing Span** 71′ **Speed** 182 knots.
Powered by 4 Gypsy Queen Air Cooled engines.

Sea Devon C Mk 20 [bottom]
Crew 2 **Length** 39′ **Height** 13′ **Wing Span** 57′ **Speed** 205 knots.
Powered by 2 Gypsy Queen Air cooled engines.

At the end of the line . . .

Readers may well find other warships afloat which are not mentioned in this book. The majority have fulfilled a long and useful life and are now relegated to non-seagoing duties. The following list gives details of their current duties:

Penn. No.	Ship	Remarks
A134	RAME HEAD	Maintenance Ship. Used as an Accommodation Ship at Portsmouth
A191	BERRY HEAD	As above, but at Devonport
C35	BELFAST	World War II Cruiser On permanent display — Pool of London.
D73	CAVALIER	World War II Destroyer. Museum Ship at Southampton. (open to the public)
F32	SALISBURY	Cathedral Class Frigate Harbour Training and Accommodation Ship at Devonport.
F48 & F54	DUNDAS & HARDY	Captain Class Frigates Accommodation Ships at Portsmouth.
F73 & F80	EASTBOURNE & DUNCAN	Type 12 & Captain Class Frigates — Both Engineers Harbour Training Ships at Rosyth.
F97 & F117	RUSSELL & ASHANTI	Captain & Tribal Class Frigates — Engineers Harbour Training Ships at Gosport
S05	FINWHALE	Porpoise Class Submarine Harbour Training Ship at Gosport.
S67	ALLIANCE	Submarine Museum Ship at Gosport. (open to the public)

At the time of publishing the following ships were awaiting tow for scrap or sale.

PORTSMOUTH	PLYMOUTH	CHATHAM	
Reclaim (A231)	Forth (A187)		Blake (C99)
Tiger (C20)	Narwhal (S03)		Lincoln (F99)
Devonshire (D02)			Brighton (F106)
Palliser (F94)			Berwick (F115)
Grenville (F197)			Mohawk (F125)
Bulwark (R08)			